Monday	Tuesday	Wednesday	Thursday
Friday	Saturday	Sunday	

CU01306285

Monday	Tuesday	Wednesday	Thursday
Friday	Saturday	Sunday	

Monday	Tuesday	Wednesday	Thursday
Friday	Saturday	Sunday	

Monday	Tuesday	Wednesday	Thursday
Friday	**Saturday**	**Sunday**	

Monday	Tuesday	Wednesday	Thursday
Friday	Saturday	Sunday	

Monday	Tuesday	Wednesday	Thursday

Friday	Saturday	Sunday	
			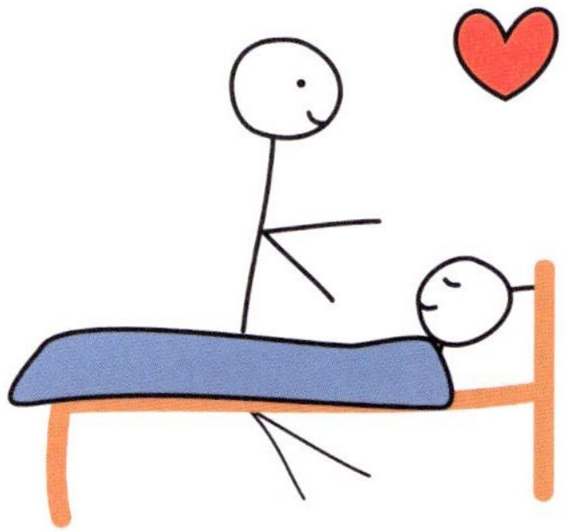

Monday	Tuesday	Wednesday	Thursday
Friday	Saturday	Sunday	

Monday	Tuesday	Wednesday	Thursday
Friday	Saturday	Sunday	

Monday	Tuesday	Wednesday	Thursday
Friday	**Saturday**	**Sunday**	

Monday	Tuesday	Wednesday	Thursday
Friday	Saturday	Sunday	

Monday	Tuesday	Wednesday	Thursday
Friday	Saturday	Sunday	

Monday	Tuesday	Wednesday	Thursday

Friday	Saturday	Sunday	
			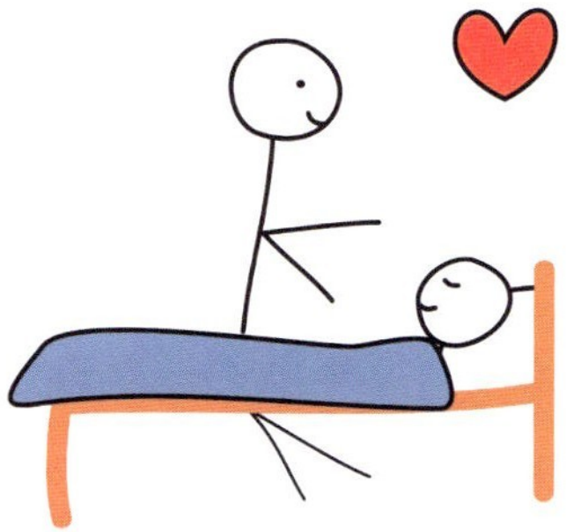

Monday	Tuesday	Wednesday	Thursday
Friday	Saturday	Sunday	

Monday	Tuesday	Wednesday	Thursday
Friday	Saturday	Sunday	

Monday	Tuesday	Wednesday	Thursday
Friday	Saturday	Sunday	

Monday	Tuesday	Wednesday	Thursday
Friday	Saturday	Sunday	

Monday	Tuesday	Wednesday	Thursday
Friday	**Saturday**	**Sunday**	

Monday	Tuesday	Wednesday	Thursday
Friday	**Saturday**	**Sunday**	

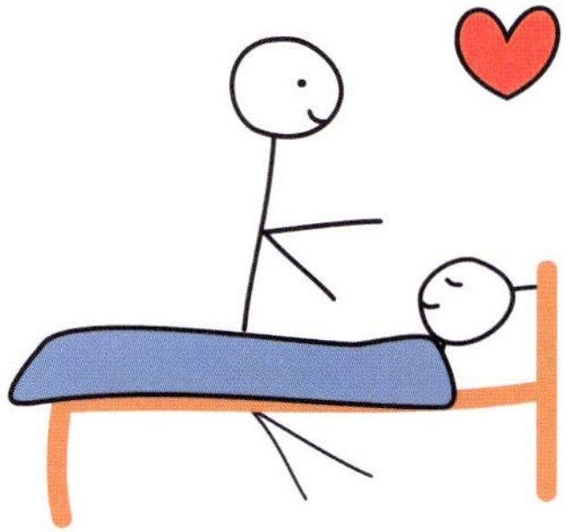

Monday	Tuesday	Wednesday	Thursday
Friday	**Saturday**	**Sunday**	

Monday	Tuesday	Wednesday	Thursday
Friday	Saturday	Sunday	

Monday	Tuesday	Wednesday	Thursday
Friday	Saturday	Sunday	

Monday	Tuesday	Wednesday	Thursday
Friday	**Saturday**	**Sunday**	

Monday	Tuesday	Wednesday	Thursday
Friday	**Saturday**	**Sunday**	

Monday	Tuesday	Wednesday	Thursday
Friday	**Saturday**	**Sunday**	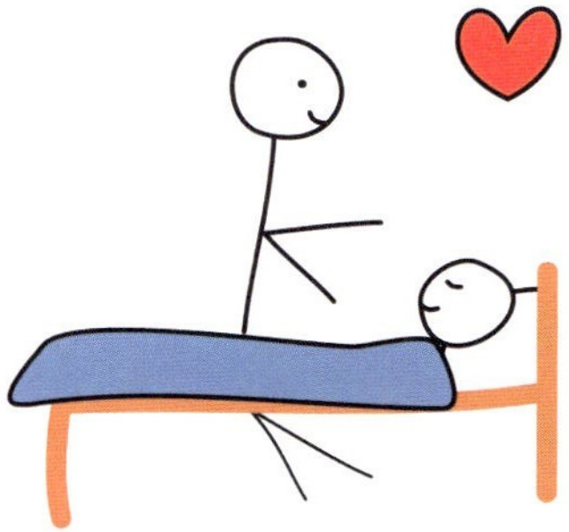

Monday	Tuesday	Wednesday	Thursday
Friday	Saturday	Sunday	

Monday	Tuesday	Wednesday	Thursday
Friday	Saturday	Sunday	

Monday	Tuesday	Wednesday	Thursday
Friday	Saturday	Sunday	

Monday	Tuesday	Wednesday	Thursday

Friday	Saturday	Sunday	

Monday	Tuesday	Wednesday	Thursday

Friday	Saturday	Sunday	

Monday	Tuesday	Wednesday	Thursday
Friday	Saturday	Sunday	
			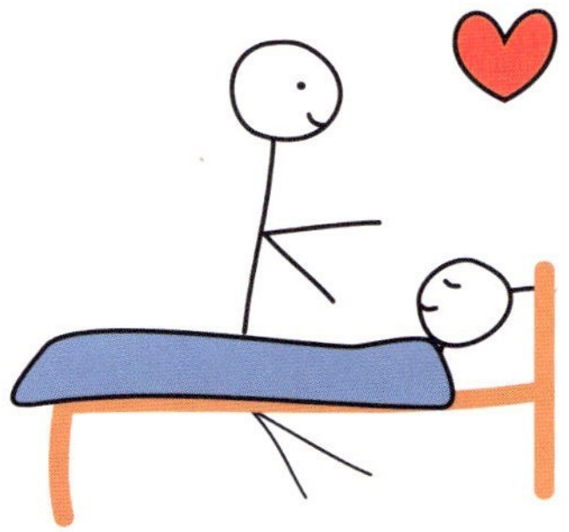

Monday	Tuesday	Wednesday	Thursday
Friday	Saturday	Sunday	

Monday	Tuesday	Wednesday	Thursday
Friday	**Saturday**	**Sunday**	

Monday	Tuesday	Wednesday	Thursday
Friday	**Saturday**	**Sunday**	

Monday

Tuesday

Wednesday

Thursday

Friday

Saturday

Sunday

Monday	Tuesday	Wednesday	Thursday

Friday	Saturday	Sunday	

Monday	Tuesday	Wednesday	Thursday
Friday	**Saturday**	**Sunday**	
			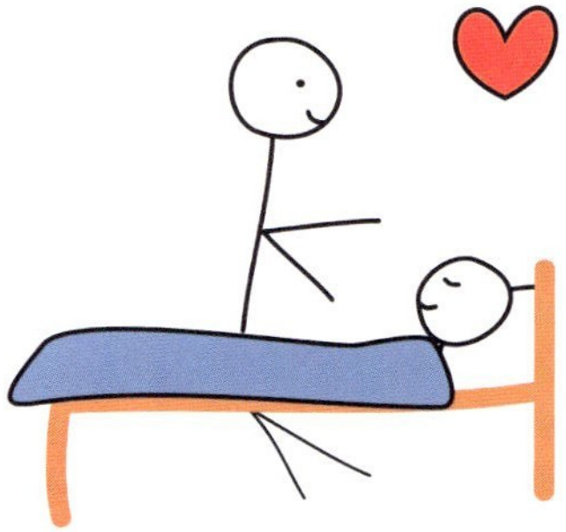

Monday	Tuesday	Wednesday	Thursday
Friday	Saturday	Sunday	

Monday	Tuesday	Wednesday	Thursday
Friday	Saturday	Sunday	

Monday	Tuesday	Wednesday	Thursday
Friday	Saturday	Sunday	

Monday	Tuesday	Wednesday	Thursday
Friday	**Saturday**	**Sunday**	

Monday	Tuesday	Wednesday	Thursday

Friday	Saturday	Sunday	

Monday	Tuesday	Wednesday	Thursday
Friday	**Saturday**	**Sunday**	
			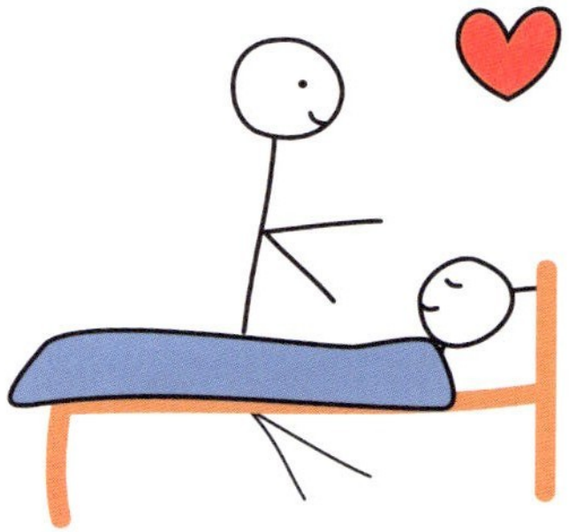

Monday	Tuesday	Wednesday	Thursday
Friday	Saturday	Sunday	

Monday	Tuesday	Wednesday	Thursday
Friday	Saturday	Sunday	

Monday	Tuesday	Wednesday	Thursday
Friday	Saturday	Sunday	

Monday	Tuesday	Wednesday	Thursday

Friday	Saturday	Sunday	

Monday	Tuesday	Wednesday	Thursday

Friday	Saturday	Sunday	

Monday	Tuesday	Wednesday	Thursday
Friday	**Saturday**	**Sunday**	
			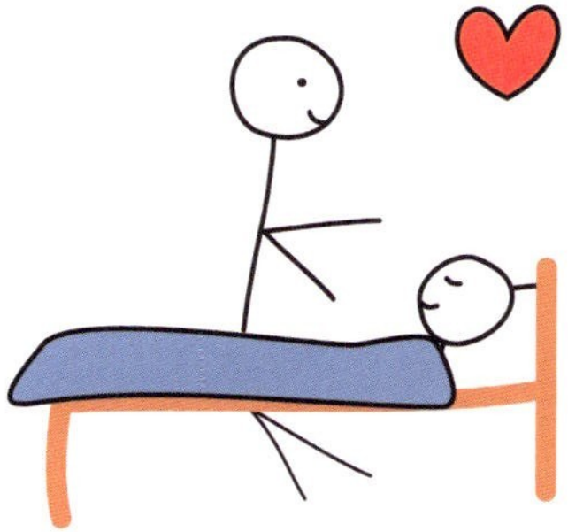

Monday	Tuesday	Wednesday	Thursday
Friday	**Saturday**	**Sunday**